GW00503793

Published in 2012 by Helen Exley Giftbooks in
Great Britain.

Design, selection and arrangement copyright
© Helen Exley Creative Ltd 2012.
Illustrations copyright © Helen Exley Creative Ltd
2012.
The moral right of the author has been asserted.

12 11 10 9 8 7 6 5 4 3 2 1

ISBN 978-1-84634-631-6

Helen Exley Giftbooks,
16 Chalk Hill, Watford, Herts WD19 4BG, UK.

www.helenexleygiftbooks.com

...so in love!

ILLUSTRATIONS BY ANGELA KERR

A HELEN EXLEY GIFTBOOK

OTHER HELEN EXLEY GIFTBOOKS

Love... I See Only You

Marriage. The Great Gift.

I Love You Madly

To my very special Love

Shakespeare on Love

To my fabulous Man

ABOUT THIS BOOK

...*So In Love is an unashamed collection of the most romantic, crazy words ever written by the world's most idiotic, unhinged people in love. Writers, from Sophocles to Shakespeare, from Goethe to Wordsworth,*

*lay it all out: the
tumultuous emotions
most of us are attacked by –
if we are lucky –
at least once in our lives.
Helen Exley says of this
bumper little collection,
"These are the most
superb quotes from
the world's most brilliant
writers. Enjoy!"*

Love is a short word,
but it contains all:
it means the body, the soul,
the life, the entire being.

GUY DE MAUPASSANT
(1850-1893)

In our life there is a single
color, as on an artist's palette,
which provides the meaning
of life and art.
It is the color of love.

MARC CHAGALL
(1889-1985)

You cannot touch love either; but you feel the sweetness that it pours into everything.

ANNIE SULLIVAN
(1866-1936)

*We feel it as we feel
the warmth of the blood,
we breathe it as
we breathe the air,
we carry it in ourselves
as we carry our thoughts...
it is an inexpressible
state indicated
by four letters....*

GUY DE MAUPASSANT
(1850-1893)

*L*ove alone is capable
of uniting living beings
in such a way as to complete
and fulfil them, for it alone
takes them and joins
them by what is deepest
in themselves.

PIERRE TEILHARD DE CHARDIN

*Oh, the comfort –
the inexpressible
comfort, of feeling safe
with a person – having
neither to weigh thoughts
nor measure words,
but pouring them out.*

DINAH MARIA MULOCK CRAIK
(1820-1887)

Across the gateway
of my heart I wrote
"No thoroughfare,"
But love came
laughing by, and cried
"I enter everywhere".

HERBERT SHIPMAN

*All the wonder
and wealth of the mine
in the heart of one gem:
In the core of one pearl
all the shade and the shine
of the sea; Breath and bloom,
shade and shine...
Brightest truth, purest
trust in the universe –
all were for me. In the kiss
of one girl.*

ROBERT BROWNING
(1812-1889)

The moment we
indulge our affections,
the earth is
metamorphosed:
there is no winter,
and no night:
all tragedies,
all ennuis vanish;
all duties even....

RALPH WALDO
EMERSON (1803-1882)

... You came, and
the sun came after,
And the green grew
golden above; And the
flag-flowers lightened
with laughter,
And the meadow-sweet
shook with love.

ALGERNON CHARLES
SWINBURNE

Yours is the breath that
sets every new leaf aquiver.
Yours is the grace that guides
the rush of the river.
Yours is the flush and
the flame in the heart
of a flower: Life's
meaning, its music,
its pride and its power.

AUTHOR UNKNOWN

Being with you
is like walking
on a very clear
morning —
definitely
the sensation
of belonging
there.

E.B. WHITE (1899-1985)

Lovers don't finally meet somewhere. They're in each other all along.

JALAL AL-DIN RUMI
(1207-1273)

Love only is eternal, Love only does not die....

HARRY KEMP,
FROM
"THE PASSING FLOWER"

Love from one being to another can only be that two solitudes come nearer, recognize and protect and comfort each other.

HAN SUYIN
(MRS. ELIZABETH COMBER),
B.1917

Love is huddling
together for shelter
under an umbrella –
long after the rain
has stopped.

STUART AND LINDA MACFARLANE

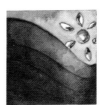

*T*o see a young couple
loving each other
is no wonder;
but to see an old couple
loving each other
is the best sight of all.

WILLIAM
MAKEPEACE THACKERAY
(1811-1863)

ANYTHING,
EVERYTHING,
LITTLE OR BIG
BECOMES AN
ADVENTURE WHEN
THE RIGHT
PERSON SHARES IT.

KATHLEEN NORRIS
(1880-1966)

Love is a wizard....
It intoxicates,
it envelops,
it isolates.
It creates fragrance
in the air, ardour
from coldness,
it beautifies
everything around it.

LEOS JANACEK
(1854-1928)

Love is enriched
by every
good thing shared
– and made stronger
by every sorrow faced
together.

PAM BROWN, B.1928

There is nothing holier, in this life of ours, than the first consciousness of love – the first fluttering of its silken wings.

HENRY WADSWORTH
LONGFELLOW
(1807-1882)

*...falling in love... is
a simultaneous firing of
two spirits engaged in the
autonomous act of growing up.
And the sensation is of
something having noiselessly
exploded inside each of them.*

LAWRENCE DURRELL
(1912-1990)

*H*ow am I to tell you
that I am intoxicated with
the faintest odour of you,
that, had I possessed you
a thousand times, you would
see me still more intoxicated,
because there would be hope
and memory where there
is as yet only hope.

HONORÉ DE BALZAC
(1799-1850),
TO HIS FUTURE WIFE EVELINE

Please suggest a remedy to stop me trembling with joy like a lunatic when I receive and read your letters....
You have given me a gift such as I never even dreamt of finding in this life.

FRANZ KAFKA (1883-1924)

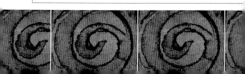

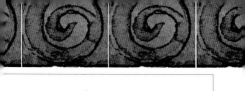

ACROSS
HOW MANY
THOUSAND MILES
I LIE TOSSING
TO YOUR
HEART BEAT.

ANDREW HARVEY,
FROM "A FULL CIRCLE"

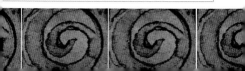

Oh, my heart
is thirsty
for your kisses...

NATHANIEL HAWTHORNE
(1804-1864),
TO HIS FIANCÉE
SOPHIA PEABODY

*O Lyric Love,
half angel and
half bird,
And all a wonder
and a wild desire!*

ROBERT BROWNING
(1812-1889)

*L*ove me
with thine
hand stretched
out. Freely
– open-minded.

ELIZABETH
BARRETT BROWNING
(1806-1861)

The breeze is blowing
Towards the open sea
at Turanga,
You are far away,
my dear
My love goes out
to you from here.

My love falls like the rain
On the open sea
at Turanga
I am left behind here
Living with my love
for you.

MAORI SONG

Only love heals,
makes whole,
takes us beyond
ourselves.

MARSHA SINETAR

Love is
the strongest of
nature's forces
– able to bring joy
even out of tragedy.

STUART AND LINDA
MACFARLANE

Love makes
all hard hearts
gentle.

GEORGE HERBERT
(1593-1633)

Our love is like
the misty rain
that falls
softly – but
floods the river.

AFRICAN PROVERB

Our meeting makes
this summer night
A new world,
with new species
and new dangers;
And we are made new
in each other's sight,
For by continual
growth, love keeps
us strangers.

JAMES MCAULEY
(1917-1976)

I am giddy; expectation
whirls me round;
Th'imaginary relish
is so sweet
That it enchants my sense.

WILLIAM SHAKESPEARE
(1564-1616)

IN YOU ALONE
MY DESIRES GIVE
BIRTH TO
DELIRIUM,
IN YOU ALONE
MY LOVE BATHES
IN LOVE.

PAUL ELUARD
(PAUL-EUGENE GRINDEL)
(1895-1952)

I do love
nothing in the world
so well as you;
is not that strange?

WILLIAM SHAKESPEARE
(1564-1616)

Love is
WHEN THE DESIRE
TO BE DESIRED
TAKES YOU SO BADLY
THAT YOU FEEL YOU
COULD DIE OF IT.

HENRI DE
TOULOUSE-LAUTREC
(1864-1901)

Their lips drew
near, and clung
into a kiss;
A long, long kiss,
a kiss of youth
and love...
Each kiss a
heart-quake....

LORD BYRON
(1788-1824),
FROM "DON JUAN"

Love vanquishes time.
To lovers,
a moment can be eternity,
eternity can be
the tick of a clock.

MARY PARRISH
(PSEUDONYM OF
MARGARET COUSINS)

A LETTER
FROM YOU,
AND THE
UNIVERSE
(THAT'S ME)
SINGS.

MALCOLM LOWRY,
TO JAN GABRIAL

You cannot believe
how much I miss you.
I stay awake most of the night
thinking of you, and by day
I find my feet carrying me...
to your room... then finding
it empty I depart,
as sick and sorrowful as
a lover locked out.

PLINY THE YOUNGER,
(1ST CENTURY A.D.),
TO HIS WIFE CALPURNIA

'Tis love that
makes me bold
and resolute, Love
that can find
a way where path
there's none,
Of all the gods
the most invincible.

EURIPIDES
(480-406 B.C.)

You've been in love; you know what it's like. It's a sense of delight, not just in the person you love, but in all people, in yourself, in life. Suddenly you see beauty, excitement everywhere.

You're not afraid to
express your love:
passionately,
gently, in words,
or in silence.
And you feel
strong, generous,
fully alive.

GEORGE WEINBERG

To love
is the great Amulet
that makes this
world a garden.

ROBERT LOUIS STEVENSON
(1850-1894)

I love the scent of your hair – I love to touch it with my lips and feel it upon my face. See, I kiss it here on the moonbeam that marks its parting: and I lay my face into its coiled masses as one might smell a mass of clustered violets.

ROBERT BURDETTE,
TO HIS FUTURE WIFE CLARA

To me you are the gate of paradise. For you I will renounce fame, creativity, everything.

FREDERIC CHOPIN
(1810-1849),
TO HIS MISTRESS
DELPHINE POTOCKA

I think you are good, gifted, lovely: a fervent, a solemn passion is conceived in my heart; it leans to you, draws you to my centre and spring of life, wraps my existence about you – and, kindling in pure, powerful flame, fuses you and me in one.

CHARLOTTE BRONTE
(1816-1855)

Love is
that condition
in which
the happiness
of another person
is essential
to your own.

ROBERT HEINLEIN

*L*ove is not "blind"
but visionary:
it sees into the very heart
of its object,
and sees the "real self"
behind and in
the midst of the frailties
and shortcomings
of the person.

ANDRAS ANGYAL

For love is but
the heart's
immortal thirst
to be completely
known and all
forgiven.

HENRY VAN DYKE
(1852-1933)

It takes a lot
of courage
to show
your dreams to
someone else.

ERMA BOMBECK
(1927-1996)

LOVE IS
NEVER HAVING
TO SAY
YOU'RE SORRY.

ERICH SEGAL, B.1937

Do WHAT YOU WILL.
IGNORE IT. NEGLECT IT.
STARVE IT. IT'S STRONGER
THAN BOTH OF US
TOGETHER.

FROM "NOW, VOYAGER"

*The sound of a kiss
is not so loud as that of
a cannon, but its echo lasts
a great deal longer.*

OLIVER WENDELL HOLMES
(1809-1894)

*Scientists can write
all the books they like
about love being a trap
of nature....
But all that scientists
are going to
convince are other scientists,
not women in love.*

JEAN ARTHUR, AS MARY JONES, FROM
"THE DEVIL AND MISS JONES"

There is no greater
wonder than the way
the face of a young woman
fits in a man's mind,
and stays there,
and he could never tell
you why; it just seems it
was the thing he wanted.

ROBERT LOUIS STEVENSON
(1850-1894)

*The best and
most beautiful
things in the world
cannot be seen
or even touched.
They must be felt
with the heart.*

HELEN KELLER
(1880-1968)

*S*weet is snow in summer
for the thirsty to drink,
and sweet for sailors
after winter to see
the garland of spring;
but most sweet
when one cloak shelters
two lovers, and the tale
of love is told by both.

ASCLEPIADES
(FL. 3RD CENTURY B.C.)

Familiar acts are beautiful through love.

PERCY BYSSHE SHELLEY
(1792-1822),
FROM "PROMETHEUS UNBOUND"

Love is but the discovery of ourselves in others, and the delight in the recognition.

ALEXANDER SMITH
(1830-1867),
FROM "DREAMTHORP"

*Romance is an
eager striving always
to appear attractive
to each other.... Love
is two people who find beauty
in each other
no matter how they look.*

MARJORIE HOLMES, B.1910

*L*ove means to commit
oneself without guarantee,
to give oneself completely
in the hope that
our love will produce love
in the loved person.
Love is an act
of faith, and whoever
is of little faith
is also of little love.

ERICH FROMM (1900-1980)

*'Tis love, 'tis love,
that makes the world
go round!*

LEWIS CARROLL
(1832-1898),
FROM "ALICE'S ADVENTURES
IN WONDERLAND"

Love is rarely
to be found in
extravagant gestures.
It is mostly
revealed in a quiet word
or a gentle smile.

STUART AND LINDA
MACFARLANE

*N*ever forget
*that the most
powerful force on earth
is Love.*

NELSON ROCKEFELLER
(1908-1979)

COUPLES WHO
LOVE EACH OTHER
TELL EACH OTHER
A THOUSAND THINGS
WITHOUT TALKING.

CHINESE PROVERB

You know how it is
when it happens, like a search
that's ended. And the
wonderful relief at having
found someone to go home
and talk to, who knows
you, understands your
work and everything
you're going through.

DERVLA KIRWAN

I met in the street
a very poor young man
who was in love.
His hat was old, his coat worn,
his cloak was out at
the elbows, the water
passed through his shoes, –
and the stars through
his soul.

VICTOR HUGO (1802-1885)

...it seemed to me that
I had known her for a long
time, and that before her
I had known nothing
and had not lived...
"And here I am sitting
opposite her," I was
thinking, "I have met her;
I know her. God, what
happiness!" I almost leapt
from my chair in ecstasy....

IVAN TURGENEV
(1818-1883)

I F I WERE PRESSED
TO SAY WHY I LOVE HIM,
I FEEL THAT MY ONLY
REPLY COULD BE:
"BECAUSE IT WAS HE,
BECAUSE IT WAS I".

MICHEL DE MONTAIGNE
(1533-1592)

Love makes bitter things sweet; love converts base copper to gold. By love dregs become clear; by love pains

become healing.
By love the dead
are brought to life;
by love a king is made
a slave.

JALAL AL-DIN RUMI
(1207-1273)

THE WHOLE WORLD
IS A MARKET-PLACE
FOR LOVE,
FOR NAUGHT THAT IS,
FROM LOVE REMAINS
REMOTE.
THE ETERNAL WISDOM
MADE ALL
THINGS IN LOVE:

FARID AL-DIN ATTAR

*O*nly three things
are infinite:
the sky in its stars,
the sea in its drops
of water, and the
heart in its tears.

GUSTAVE FLAUBERT
(1821-1880)

All of life
is divided into
three periods:
the premonition
of love, the action
of love, and
the recollection
of love.

MARIA TSVETAYEVA
(1892-1941)

*A*ll, everything
that I understand,
I understand only
because I love.

LEO TOLSTOY
(1828-1910),
FROM
"WAR AND PEACE"

He glared at her
a moment through the dusk,
and the next instant she felt
his arms about her and his
lips on her own lips.
His kiss was like white
lightning, a flash that spread,
and spread again,
and stayed.

HENRY JAMES (1843-1916),
FROM
"THE PORTRAIT OF A LADY"

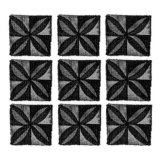

*Time is too slow
for those who wait,
too swift for those who
fear, too long for those
who grieve, too short
for those who rejoice,
but for those who love,
time is eternity.*

HENRY VAN DYKE

My love, my angel, you are gone. You were able to go away and leave me for six months! No, I shall never resist the tedium of so long an absence. It has lasted only four hours and is already insupportable.

MADAME D'EPINAY,
TO HER HUSBAND

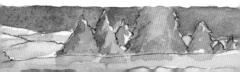

THIS MORNING
*The sun must have climbed
round the edge of the window
this morning – caressing
my face, and sleep filled eyes
ever so tenderly –*

*For, (in the fleeting wistful
waking moments), I thought
I prayed that the gentle
warmth could be you...*

R.M. GOMM

*Fill your paper
with the breathings
of your heart....*

WILLIAM WORDSWORTH
(1770-1850),
TO HIS WIFE MARY

When Love speaks,
the voice of all the gods
Makes heaven drowsy
with the harmony.

WILLIAM SHAKESPEARE
(1564-1616),
FROM "LOVE'S LABOUR'S LOST", IV: III

...the world was newly crowned with flowers, when first we met.

THOMAS HOOD
(1799-1845),
FROM "THE TIME OF ROSES"

*Love is...
...second life, it grows
into the soul
Warms every vein,
and beats in every pulse.*

JOSEPH ADDISON
(1672-1719)

I DON'T WANT TO LIVE – I WANT TO LOVE FIRST, AND LIVE INCIDENTALLY.

ZELDA FITZGERALD
(1900-1948),
TO F. SCOTT FITZGERALD

...we are made
for loving: all
the sweets of
living are for
those that love.
Be joyful,
unafraid!

THE RUBAIYAT
OF OMAR KHAYYAM
(C.1048– C.1122)

*One word
frees us of all
the weight and
pain of life:
That word
is love.*

SOPHOCLES
(496-406 B.C.)

When one has once
fully entered the realm of love,
the world – no matter
how imperfect – becomes rich
and beautiful,
for it consists solely of
opportunities for love.

SOREN KIERKEGAARD
(1813-1855)

There are no little
events with the heart.
It magnifies everything;
it places in the same scales
the fall of an empire
of fourteen years and
the dropping of a woman's
glove, and almost always
the glove weighs more
than the empire.

HONORÉ DE BALZAC
(1799-1850)

THE HEART'S FRIEND

Fair is the white star of twilight,
and the sky cleaner
At the day's end;
But she is fairer, and she is dearer,
She, my heart's friend!

Fair is the white star of twilight,
And the moon roving
To the sky's end;
But she is fairer, better worth
loving, She, my heart's friend.

SHOSHONE LOVE SONG

*I could die for you.
My creed is love
and you are its
only tenet.
You have ravish'd
me away by power
I cannot resist....
I cannot breathe
without you.*

JOHN KEATS
(1795-1821),
TO FANNY BRAWNE

THERE'S NOTHING MORE PRECIOUS IN THIS WORLD THAN THE FEELING OF BEING WANTED.

DIANA DORS (1931-1984)

He was comforted
by one of the simpler
emotions which some
human beings are lucky
enough to experience.
He knew when
he died he would be
watched by someone
he loved.

NOEL ANNAN, ON E.M. FORSTER

*T*o-day a new sun rises
for me; everything lives,
everything is animated,
everything seems to speak
to me of my passion,
everything invites me
to cherish it.
The fire consuming me gives
to my heart, to all the faculties
of my soul, a resilience,
an activity....

NINON DE L'ENCLOS
(1616-1706), TO THE MARQUIS
DE SEVIGNY

...I come apart
in your hands
like pieces of a
vast and unsolved
puzzle.

LINDA PASTAN,
B.1932

THE CRY OF MY BODY
FOR COMPLETENESS,
THAT IS A CRY TO YOU.

MARY CAROLYN DAVIES

*There shall be such
a oneness between you
that when one weeps,
the other shall taste salt.*

PROVERB

*T*HERE IS ONLY
ONE HAPPINESS
IN LIFE, TO LOVE
AND BE LOVED.

GEORGE SAND
(AMANDINE AURORE LUCIE DUPIN)
(1804-1876)

*C*herish me with
that dignified tenderness
which I have only found
in you...

MARY WOLLSTONECRAFT
(1759-1797)

...YOUR FACE
AFTER LOVE,
CLOSE
TO THE PILLOW,
A LULLABY.

ANNE SEXTON
(1928-1974)

Lay in my arms till
break of day then tarry
a little while longer.

LINDA MACFARLANE, B.1953

Only he felt
he could no
more dissemble
And kissed her,
mouth to
mouth, all in
a tremble.

LEIGH HUNT
(1784-1859), FROM "STORY
OF RIMINI"

Romantic love "happens"; it is not brought about; one falls in love. The person is obsessed with the loved one and is unable to concentrate on anything else. The person loses all desire to remain independent, and instead desires to merge and subsume... into the other.

MARGARET HORTON

*L*ove...
it will put its hook
into your heart
and force you to know
that of all strong things
nothing is so strong,
so irresistible,
as divine love.

WILLIAM LAW (1686-1761)

*Two lovely berries
moulded on one stem:
So, with two
seeming bodies,
but one heart.*

WILLIAM SHAKESPEARE
(1564-1616),
FROM "A MIDSUMMER NIGHT'S DREAM"

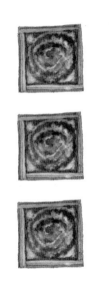

I CAN NEITHER
EAT NOR SLEEP
FOR THINKING
OF YOU
MY DEAREST LOVE,
I NEVER TOUCH
EVEN PUDDING.

HORATIO NELSON
(1758-1805),
TO LADY EMMA HAMILTON

Doubt thou the stars
are fire;
Doubt that the sun
doth move;
Doubt truth to be a liar;
But never doubt I love.

WILLIAM SHAKESPEARE
(1564-1616),
FROM "HAMLET"

*Jack, I shan't hide
what I feel today.
I woke up with you
in my breast and on
my lips. Jack, I love
you terribly today.
The whole world
is gone.
There is only you.*

*I walk about, dress,
eat, write – but all
the time I am
breathing you.*

KATHERINE MANSFIELD
(1888-1923),
TO JOHN MIDDLETON MURRY

The sun cannot shine
without you, the birds
can make no melody.
The flowers have no
other beauty or perfume –
all is a meaningless waste.
I love you darling....
You are in every thought,
dream, hope, desire.

AUSTIN DICKINSON
(1829-1895), IN A LETTER
TO MABEL TODD

Love is,
above all,
the gift
of oneself.

JEAN ANOUILH
(1910-1987)

ALONE
IN A CROWD
I CAN FEEL
ISOLATED
IN SECRET JOY
JUST THINKING
OF HIM.

N. PAYNE

I am loved:
a message
clanging of a bell
in silence.

JOYCE CAROL OATES,
B.1938,
FROM "HOW GENTLE"

OLIVIA: How does
he love me?
VIOLA: With
adorations,
fertile tears,
With groans that
thunder love,
with sighs of fire.

WILLIAM SHAKESPEARE
(1564-1616),
FROM "TWELFTH NIGHT"

I HAVE SEEN ONLY YOU,
I HAVE ADMIRED
ONLY YOU,
I DESIRE ONLY YOU.

NAPOLEON BONAPARTE
(1769-1821)

*I'd rather face failure
with you beside me than
success with anyone else.*

JENNY DE VRIES
(1947-1991)

I shall fold my arms together,
after I am in bed, and try to
imagine that you are close to my
heart. Naughty wife, what right
have you to be anywhere else?
How many sweet words
I should breathe into your ear,
in the quiet night – how many
holy kisses would I press upon
your lips....

NATHANIEL HAWTHORNE (1804-1864)

*Long as I live, my heart
will never vary
For no one else,
however fair or good
Brave, resolute
or rich, of gentle blood,
My choice is made,
and I will have no other.*

FRENCH POEM
(15/16TH CENTURY)

If I had never met him I would have dreamed him into being.

ANZIA YEZIERSKA
(1885-1970)

He came to me with
the most wonderful
tenderness. He was afraid
and I was afraid, but there
it was, that openness:
he was as delicate and fragile
and beautiful as a flower,
the blossom trembling in
full bloom....

VICTORIA FREEMAN

Love –
BITTERSWEET,
IRREPRESSIBLE –
LOOSENS MY LIMBS
AND I TREMBLE.

SAPPHO
(C. 655-610 B.C.)

Thou art
to me
a delicious
torment.

RALPH WALDO EMERSON
(1803-1882)

...everything you do souses me, terrifies me, tortures me, elates me, everything you do is perfect.

PAUL ELUARD
(PAUL-EUGENE GRINDEL)
(1895-1952)

A KISS IS
A LOVELY TRICK
DESIGNED BY NATURE
TO STOP SPEECH
WHEN WORDS BECOME
SUPERFLUOUS.

INGRID BERGMAN
(1915-1982)

Every kiss provokes
another. Ah, in those earliest
days of love how naturally
the kisses spring into life.
How closely, in their
abundance, are they pressed
one against another;
until lovers would find it
as hard to count the kisses
exchanged in an hour,
as to count the flowers in
a meadow in May.

MARCEL PROUST
(1871-1922)

*...and remember, each
moment I am robbed of you,
each night and all nights
I am turned away from you,
turned out by you, give me
pangs the exquisiteness
of which must be measured
by the knowledge that
they are moments and nights
lost, lost, lost forever.*

JACK LONDON (1876-1916),
TO HIS FUTURE
WIFE CHARMIAN KITTERIDGE

The day is cold and dark.
The only ray that comes
to me, the sole source
of light and warmth,
is my memory of you,
dear Marie. I think back
to our awakenings
in Como and Florence...
I feel I have
forgotten how to live.

FRANZ LISZT (1811-1886),
TO MARIE DE FLAVIGNY, COMTESSE
D'AGOULT (1805-1876)

Love is comfort in sadness, quietness in tumult, rest in weariness, hope in despair.

MARION C. GARRETTY
(1917-2005)

Treasure the love you receive above all. It will survive long after your gold and good health have vanished.

OG MANDINO

Living here
far away I am yours.
Living there
far away
you are mine.
Love is not made
of bodies. Only deep
in the hearts
is where we are one.

SANSKRIT LOVE POETRY

Brief
IS LIFE
BUT LONG
IS LOVE.

ALFRED,
LORD TENNYSON
(1809-1892)

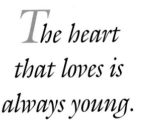

*The heart
that loves is
always young.*

GREEK PROVERB

My heart
has made its mind up
And I'm
afraid it's you.

WENDY COPE

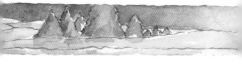

Gladly I'll live in
a poor mountain hut,
Spin, sew, and till
the soil in any weather,
And wash in the
cold mountain stream,
if but
We dwell together.

AUTHOR UNKNOWN

To love is to place our happiness in the happiness of another.

GOTTFRIED WILHELM VON LEIBNITZ
(1646-1716)

"*I can make you happy,*" *said he....* "*And at home by the fire, whenever you look up, there I shall be – and whenever I look up, there will be you.*"

THOMAS HARDY (1840-1928)

*He poured
so gently and naturally
into my life
like batter into a bowl
of batter. Honey into
a jar of honey. The clearest
water sinking into sand.*

JUSTINE SYDNEY

*I*n the arithmetic
of love, one plus one equals
everything, and two minus
one equals nothing.

MIGNON MCLAUGHLIN,
B.1915

Love does not consist
in gazing at each other
but in looking
outward together
in the same direction.

ANTOINE DE SAINT-EXUPERY
(1900-1944)

*T*his was what love was:
this consecration,
this curious uplifting,
this sudden
inexplicable joy, and this
intolerable pain....

AUTHOR UNKNOWN

How sad and bad

and mad it was –
But then,
how it was sweet!

ROBERT BROWNING
(1812-1889)

My bounty is
as boundless as the sea,
My love as deep.
The more I give to thee
The more I have,
for both are infinite.

WILLIAM SHAKESPEARE
(1564-1616)
FROM "ROMEO AND JULIET"

I kiss your hands and kneel before you... to assure you that my whole mind, all the breadth of my spirit, all my heart exist only to love you. I adore you... so beautiful, so perfect, so made to be cherished, adored and loved to death and madness.

PRINCESS
CAROLYNE JEANNE ELISABETH
VON SAYNWITTGENSTEIN

Love is a pardonable insanity.

SEBASTIEN CHAMFORT
(1741-1794)

Wild nights are my glory....

MADELEINE L'ENGLE,
B.1918

*L*ove is
supposed to be
as effortless
as breathing
and as lovely as
fallen snow
– and it is.

JULIE KRONE, B.1963

The dictionary says that a kiss is "a salute made by touching with the lips pressed closely together and suddenly parting them." From this it is quite obvious that,

although a dictionary
may know something
about words,
it knows nothing
about kissing.

HUGH MORRIS, FROM
"THE ART OF KISSING"

*I*ntensity of attraction
is a beautiful thing.
But to mislabel it love is
both foolish and dangerous.
What love requires on top
of instant emotion is time,
shared experiences and
feelings, and a long
and tempered bond between
two people.

STANTON PEELE

*P*laces that are
empty of you...
are empty of all life.

DANTE GABRIEL ROSSETTI
(1828-1882)

I ARISE FROM
DREAMS OF THEE
IN THE FIRST SWEET
SLEEP OF NIGHT,
WHEN THE WINDS
ARE BREATHING LOW,
AND THE STARS ARE
SHINING BRIGHT.

PERCY BYSSHE SHELLEY
(1792-1822)

Numberless insects
there are that call from
dawn to evening, Crying
"I love! I love!"
But the firefly's silent
passion, Making its
body burn, is deeper
than all their longing.
Even such is my love....

JAPANESE TRADITIONAL SONG

My tangled hair
I shall not cut:
Your hand,
my dearest,
Touched it as
a pillow.

JAPANESE VERSE

Two that have loved, and now divided far, Bound by loves bond, in heart together are.

WALOFRED STRABO (809-849)

Once again last night
you would not let me sleep.
Before I went to sleep
I moved over and made
room for you and tried
to imagine you there so
soft and warm and smooth.
I put out a hand
and was disappointed.

BOB GRAFTON,
TO HIS FUTURE WIFE DOT

LOVE IS A FLOWER
SO DELICATE THAT A TOUCH
WILL BRUISE IT, SO STRONG
THAT NOTHING WILL STOP
ITS GROWTH.

FERN WHEELER

Two things cannot alter,
Since Time was, nor today:
The flowing of water;
And Love's
strange, sweet way.

JAPANESE LYRIC

I have learned
not to worry about love;
but to honor its coming
with all my heart.

ALICE WALKER, B.1944

*I*s it so small a thing
 To have enjoyed
 the sun,
To have lived light
 in the spring,
To have loved,
to have thought,
to have done?

MATTHEW ARNOLD
(1822-1888)

Having someone wonder where you are when you don't come home at night is a very old human need.

MARGARET MEAD
(1901-1978)

*I*n fact, though their acquaintance had been so short, they had guessed, as always happens between lovers, everything of any importance about each other in two seconds at the utmost....

VIRGINIA WOOLF (1882-1941)

They loved...
their souls kissed,
they kissed
with their eyes,
they were
both but one
single kiss.

HEINRICH HEINE (1797-1856)

Breathless,
we flung us on
the windy hill,
Laughed
in the sun,
and kissed the
lovely grass.

RUPERT BROOKE
(1887-1915)

*Now love the
limb-loosener
sweeps me away....*

SAPPHO (C. 655-610 B.C.)

I seemed to have only
black-and-white memories
before me.
But when you came
you brought laughter,
red balloons,
silly surprises, fizz
and JOY into my life.

JUDITH C. GRANT,
B.1960

*I am just walking around
here between the lines
[of my letter], under the
light of your eyes,
in the breath of your mouth
as in a
beautiful happy day.*

FRANZ KAFKA (1883-1924)

...for two days,
I have been asking
myself every moment
if such happiness is not
a dream. It seems to
me that what
I feel is not of earth.
I cannot yet comprehend
this cloudless heaven.

VICTOR HUGO
(1802-1885),
TO ADÈLE FOUCHER

*The consciousness
of loving and
being loved brings
a warmth and richness
to life that nothing
else can bring.*

OSCAR WILDE
(1854-1900)

This is to let you know
That all that I feel
for you
Can never wholly go.
I love you and miss you,
even two hours away,
With all my heart.
This is to let you know.

NOEL COWARD
(1899-1973)

And our lips found
ways of speaking
What words
cannot say,
Till a hundred
nests gave music,
And the East
was gray.

FREDERICK LAWRENCE KNOWLES
(1869-1905)

Oh! THE HEART
THAT HAS
TRULY LOVED
NEVER FORGETS.

THOMAS MOORE
(1779-1852)

He is not a lover who does not love forever.

EURIPIDES

All loves lead
to the final love,
to the final stripping
away of the unreal selves,
to the true meeting....
It was such a miracle
that it hardly mattered
whether it was in first
or second marriage,

whether in youth or
middle age. Whenever
it happened,
it was the true meeting,
the true marriage.

ANNE MORROW LINDBERGH
(1906-2001)

Love doesn't attempt to bind, ensnare, capture. It is light, free of the burden of attachments. Love asks nothing, is fulfilled in itself. When love is there, nothing remains to be done.

VIMALA THAKAR

*While unhurried
days come and go,
Let us turn to each
other in quiet affection,
walk in peace
to the edge of old age.*

ANCIENT EGYPTIAN SONG

LOVE IS... born
with the pleasure
of looking at each
other, it is fed with
the necessity of seeing
each other, it is
concluded with the
impossibility
of separation!

JOSÉ MARTÍ Y PERÉZ
(1835-1895)

Nobody
has ever measured,
not even poets,
how much
the heart can hold.

ZELDA FITZGERALD
(1900-1948)

*S*ome day, after we have
mastered the winds,
the waves, the tides
and gravity we shall
harness the energies
of love. Then, for the
second time in the history
of the world, man will
have discovered fire.

PIERRE TEILHARD DE CHARDIN
(1881-1955)

*T*he entire sum
of existence
is the magic
of being needed
by just one person.

V. PUTNAM

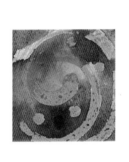

Bright glass
shatters
as do so many
memories.
But these days
are diamond
and will shine
forever.

PAM BROWN, B.1928

You SMILED
AND TALKED TO ME
OF NOTHING AND
I FELT FOR THIS
I HAD BEEN
WAITING LONG.

RABINDRANATH TAGORE
(1861-1941)

*In dreams
and in love there are
no impossibilities.*

JANUS ARONY

WHAT IS A HELEN EXLEY GIFTBOOK?

Helen Exley Giftbooks cover the most
powerful of all human relationships:
the bonds within families and
between friends, and the theme
of personal values. No expense
is spared in making sure that
each book is as meaningful a gift
as it is possible to create:
good to give, good to receive.
You have the result in your hands.
If you have loved it – tell others!
There is no power on earth like
the word-of-mouth recommendation
of friends!

Helen Exley Giftbooks
16 Chalk Hill,
Watford, Herts
WD19 4BG, UK

www.helenexleygiftbooks.com

Illustrations by Angela Kerr
and editing © Helen Exley Creative Ltd. 2012
All words from Helen Exley's
collection of love quotations.